# THE
# ECHO EFFECT
## Level Up Your Respect

## CHIP KENDALL

AN IMPRINT OF
Grace & Down Publishing
malcolm down PUBLISHING

LEVEL UP BOOKS

Copyright © 2026 Chip Kendall

First published 2026 by Grace and Down Publishing Ltd an imprint of Malcolm Down Publishing
www.malcolmdown.co.uk

28 27 26 25   6 5 4 3 2 1

The right of Chip Kendall to be identified as the author of this work has been asserted by him in accordance with the Copyright, Designs and Patents Act 1988.

All rights reserved. No part of this publication may be reproduced, stored in a retrieval system, or transmitted in any other form or by any means, electronic, mechanical, photocopying, recording or otherwise, without the prior permission of the publisher.

**British Library Cataloguing in Publication Data**
A catalogue record for this book is available from the British Library.

ISBN 978-1-917455-28-2 *The Echo Effect – Level Up Your Respect*

Scripture quotations are taken from the Holy Bible, New International Version (Anglicised edition). Copyright © 1979, 1984, 2011 Biblica. Used by permission of Hodder & Stoughton Ltd, an Hachette UK company.
All rights reserved.

Cover design and illustrations by Hannah Joy Williams
Art direction by Sarah Grace
Level Up Logo Design by Joe Dunys

Printed in the UK

# ENDORSEMENTS

"This is a much needed series which will empower, validate and encourage a generation of children and families. It's inspiringly full of fun, faith & facts. I can't wait to read it with my daughter!"

*Gemma Hunt, CBeebies Presenter and Author*

"This punchy, pithy, and power-packed book is a brilliant call to action for the rising generation. It inspires kids to recognise their God-given potential, step out with confidence, and partner with Jesus to bring light, life, and love to the world around them. Every page champions creativity, courage, and the truth that every child is made on purpose for a purpose."

*Matt Summerfield, Senior Leader at Zeo Church and Board of Trustees at Youthscape*

"Level Up is exactly the kind of resource today's precious young minds need. In a world that often overwhelms or distracts, these books invite curiosity, build confidence, and encourage character, all at the very age when the brilliant brain is most open to growth.

Thanks to the incredible gift of neuroplasticity, this season of life is uniquely wired for shaping thought patterns, exploring potential, and building a sense of identity that lasts. Chip's voice is fun, and wise meeting readers where they are at whilst calling them higher. Level Up isn't just a book series, it's a toolkit for life, guiding young people to see themselves and their world with fresh eyes."

*Jo Hargreaves, The Faith Filled Therapist*


As a Christian Headteacher, I can say without hesitation that these books are both timely and much needed. Chip has an incredible gift for communicating the gospel of hope and love in a way that truly connects with children. I believe these books—and the message they carry—are essential for every Christian school and home.

*Neil Garratt, Headteacher, Elworth Church of England Primary School*


The Level Up series is needed for all children to reach their full potential and discover their true value. Chip breaks down each concept into an accessible way for children to grasp and then run with for life. Full of quotes from famous people, thought provoking stories and inspiring tales this series will encourage children to aspire to more as they engage with this thought-provoking series.

*Olly Goldenberg, Children Can*

"Chip has done it again! Level Up is full of encouragement, wisdom and joy—jam-packed with tools to help children know who they are, Whose they are, and how to be light in the world around them.

As a mum, I want my kids to read it. As a children's ministry leader, I want every child I know to read it.

This series will fire up imaginations, strengthen hearts, and point a generation towards Jesus in the most fun and faith-filled way. Absolutely brilliant!"

*Shell Perris, ALIVE Kids*


This resource does exactly what it promises—it takes us up a level! It's a permission-giving laboratory where new possibilities can grow.

It's a playground where kids can learn by doing and encounter God through joy and play. It's a Chip meal on a plate—loaded with extra, unique flavours!

It's also a wake-up call to the Church, parents, and adults everywhere to inspire our kids to become world-changers. This resource deserves to go viral.

Above all, it's a training manual to help young lives live and thrive in God's unshakeable Kingdom—especially when everything around us feels shaky.

Thank you, Chip, for your love and obedience in creating this series. Church—let's wake up and level up!

*Andy Kennedy, King's Kids International*

Fantastic insights and practical steps to developing life giving character traits that lead to fulfilment and blessings. Illuminated by great stories and inspiration from the lives of wonderful role models.

*Dom Conidi – Scripture Union England and Wales*

Chip Kendall is a vibrant communicator whose energy, vision and passion shine through his writing. The Level Up series is packed full of inspiration and written in a way that will help young people grow in confidence and character.

The world we inhabit needs young people who can lead with purpose and passion and this series will equip and resource a new generation to become the change they want to see.

*Andy Wolfe, Executive Director of Education, National Society for Education (Church of England & Church in Wales)*

"Full of inspiration and encouragement for young minds. I love how it makes faith real and relevant."

*Sam Hailes, Editor, Premier Christianity magazine*

# DEDICATION

For Eden — Godly, fun and my sweetie pie til I die. Your contagious joy and energy always lights up the room.

# THANK YOU

This series wouldn't exist without a whole team of legends behind the scenes, and I want to take a moment to say a massive thank you to each one of you.

To my amazing wife, **Helen** — thank you for being willing to take the plunge with me and cheer this whole project into existence. Your faith, courage and partnership mean the world.

To **Katherine**, my brilliant sister-in-law — your early research laid the tracks before the train had even left the station. Thank you for believing in this idea from the very beginning.

To **Hannah**, your stunning illustrations and creative design ideas have brought these pages to life in ways I couldn't have imagined. You've captured the heart of Level Up in every line and colour.

To **Malcolm**, **Sarah**, **Lydia** and the whole team at Grace Down — thank you for your skill, patience and professionalism, turning words and pictures into books that kids will actually want to pick up and read.

To Pastor **Glyn**, thank you for writing such powerful forewords and always championing the next generation with such passion and purpose.

To **Gemma**, your endorsement was the fuel I didn't know I needed — thank you for your encouragement and support.

To **Joe**, thanks for such a fun logo. You smashed it out the park.

To my kids, my family, and my friends — thanks for being the inspiration, the sounding boards, and the spark that keeps me going.

And finally, to every headteacher and teacher I've ever had the privilege of working with — thank you for opening your doors and hearts to this vision of investing in the next generation. Your daily courage and care are heroic.

To every young person reading these books: I'm praying you grow in wisdom, stature and favour with God and with people. You've got this — because He's got you.

Stay bold. Stay curious. Stay kind.

— Chip

# CONTENTS

| | |
|---|---|
| Foreword | 13 |
| Introduction | 15 |
| **Chapter One:** Start the Echo | 17 |
| **Chapter Two:** Echo It Back | 25 |
| **A Lesson from History:** The Story of Rosa Parks | 31 |
| **Chapter Three:** The Greatest Echo | 35 |
| **Deep Dive:** Martin Luther King Jr. | 43 |
| **Chapter Four:** Sound of Creation | 49 |
| **Chapter Five:** Handle with Care | 57 |
| **Chapter Six:** Echo Into Tomorrow | 63 |
| **Chapter Seven:** Breaking The Echo | 75 |
| **Chapter Eight:** Words That Echo | 85 |
| **Chapter Nine:** Honour Up | 94 |
| To Parents and Teachers | 101 |

| | |
|---|---|
| Soul Children UK | 103 |
| Worship House Kids | 105 |
| Want Chip to Visit Your School or Church? | 106 |
| Ready for More? | 107 |

# FOREWORD
## by Glyn Barrett

Let's talk about echoes.

You shout something across a canyon, and what comes back? The exact same thing, only louder, bouncier and slightly more dramatic. Now imagine life works the same way: what you put out there is what comes back to you. It's true in relationships, leadership and even how we treat ourselves. Call it what you like – karma, sowing and reaping, cause and effect – but Jesus said it like this: "Do to others as you would have them do to you" (Luke 6:31).

That's not just a nice quote for your nan's fridge magnet. That's revolutionary.

In a world where online comments get nastier by the second, and "respect" often feels like an endangered species, this book is a breath of fresh air and a bit of a reality check. The Echo Effect is here to help young people realise that their words, actions and attitudes don't just disappear into thin air. They echo. They shape atmospheres. They build (or break) people. And ultimately, they define the kind of life we get to live.

I've seen this often play out in schools, churches, leadership and families. When we choose honour over sarcasm, kindness over clout, and humility over hype, we don't just become better people. We become brighter lights in a world that desperately needs them.

Chip Kendall gets this. He's got a heart for raising world-changers. Not just loud ones, but kind, curious, confident, respectful ones. This book is full of practical ways to build the habit of honour from the lunch table to the classroom to your TikTok feed. And the best bit? It's not preachy, it's punchy. It'll make you laugh, think and maybe say sorry to your little brother (if he's lucky).

Respect might not be the flashiest word out there, but trust me, it's powerful. It can heal wounds, open doors and transform futures. And it all starts with one echo. One choice. One kid who decides to speak life when others stay silent.

So read on. Let this book shape your character. And remember: the world will echo whatever you send into it. Let's make sure it's worth repeating.

*Glyn Barrett*
Senior Pastor, !Audacious Church
National Leader, Assemblies of God Great Britain

# INTRODUCTION

## What you send out comes back.

That's the power of an echo. You shout into a canyon – *HEY!* – and your voice bounces back to you. The same thing happens with respect. When you treat someone with kindness, patience or care, it doesn't just disappear. It echoes. It comes back to you, and it often spreads further than you expect.

Respect isn't just about having good manners. It's about how you see yourself, how you treat others and how you respond to the world around you. Every action, every word, every choice – it all sends out a signal. What kind of echo will you create?

This book is all about discovering the Echo Effect – how your respect can bounce back and even inspire others to do the same. You'll learn how to respect yourself, other people, the planet and even your future. And best of all, you'll see how God shows us what true respect looks like.

Are you ready to send out something worth echoing?

CHAPTER ONE

# START THE ECHO
## Respect for...myself

> "Respect yourself and others will respect you."

Confucius, 6th-century Chinese philosopher

# The Echo Effect

Lena stared at her reflection in the mirror. "Why do I always mess things up?" she muttered under her breath.

Her grandmother, who had been quietly watching, stepped closer. "Now, now," she said gently. "That's not how we speak to someone we respect."

Lena frowned. "But I keep making mistakes."

"Everyone does," Grandma said. "But respecting yourself means being kind to yourself, even when you fail. Would you talk to your best friend that way?"

Lena shook her head. "No . . . I'd try to encourage them."

Grandma smiled. "Then why not do the same for yourself?"

Lena took a deep breath. "Okay . . . I'll try."

# What is Respect?

Respect is one of the most important values we can have. It means treating something with care, value and consideration. And the first person we need to respect is ourselves!

Self-respect is about:

- Speaking kindly to ourselves, even when we make mistakes.
- Taking care of our bodies by eating well, resting and staying active.

- Setting boundaries and knowing that we deserve to be treated well.

- Believing in our potential and not giving up when things are hard.

People who respect themselves walk with confidence – not because they think they're better than others, but because they know their worth.

Take a moment to reflect:

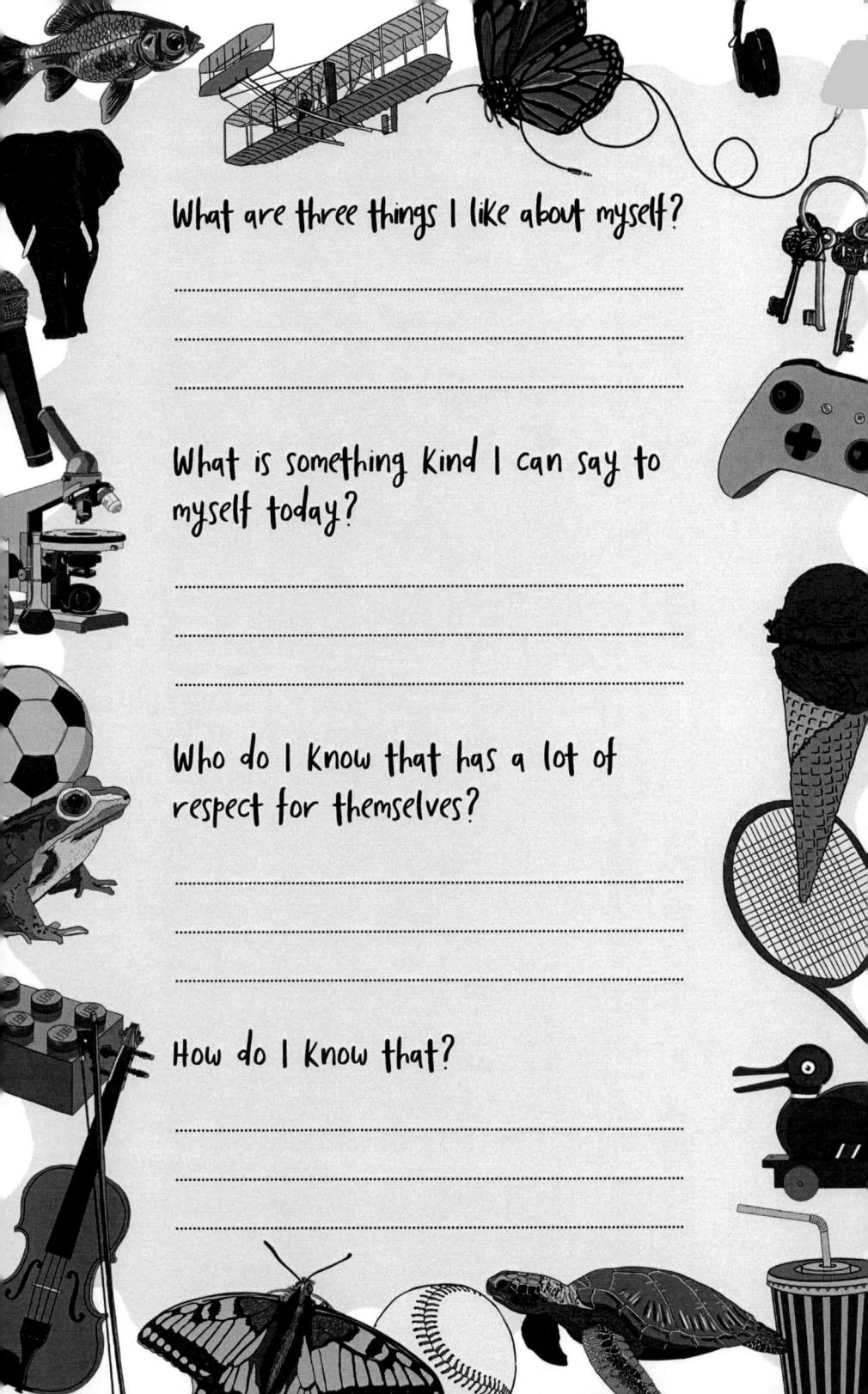

**What are three things I like about myself?**
..................................................................
..................................................................
..................................................................

**What is something kind I can say to myself today?**
..................................................................
..................................................................
..................................................................

**Who do I know that has a lot of respect for themselves?**
..................................................................
..................................................................
..................................................................

**How do I know that?**
..................................................................
..................................................................
..................................................................

# A Lesson from the Bible:
## Jesus and the Greatest Commandment

One day, a teacher of the law asked Jesus what the greatest commandment was. Jesus answered:

> *"'Love the Lord your God with all your heart and with all your soul and with all your mind.' This is the first and greatest commandment. And the second is like it: 'Love your neighbour as yourself.'"*
>
> (Matthew 22:37-39)

Many people focus on loving others, but notice what Jesus said – *love your neighbour as yourself.* That means we must also love and respect ourselves! If we don't treat ourselves with kindness, care and dignity, how can we truly do the same for others?

True self-respect isn't about being proud or thinking we are better than others. It's about knowing that we are valuable and treating ourselves in a way that honours that worth. When we respect ourselves, we are more prepared to respect and care for the people around us.

# Did You Know?

## AFRICAN ELEPHANTS AND THE MIRROR TEST

Did you know that African elephants can recognise themselves in a mirror? This test, called the **"mirror self-recognition test"**, is a rare ability that shows **self-awareness** – the understanding that you are a unique individual.

Scientists discovered this by placing a **mark on an elephant's forehead** – somewhere it could only be seen in a mirror. Instead of thinking the reflection was another elephant, the elephant **touched the mark on its own forehead**, proving it recognised itself! Very few animals can do this – only great apes, dolphins, magpies and elephants have passed the test.

Elephants show us that **respect starts with knowing our own worth.** When we value ourselves, we make good choices, stand up for what's right, and treat others with kindness.

CHAPTER TWO

# ECHO IT BACK
## Respect for...others

> "Treat people as if they were what they ought to be, and you help them become what they are capable of being."

Johann Wolfgang von Goethe,
18th-century writer

# The Echo Effect

Jordan sat nervously in the school hall as the headteacher, Mrs Patel, stepped onto the stage.

"We have a very special award to give today," she announced, smiling warmly. "This student has shown kindness, patience and respect to both classmates and teachers alike. They go out of their way to help others and always treat people with dignity. That's the kind of respect that makes a school – and the world – a better place."

Jordan's heart pounded. Was she talking about him?

Mrs Patel looked straight at him and said, "Jordan, please come up here."

Stunned, he rose to his feet as his classmates clapped. As he walked to the stage, he thought about the times he'd stood up for his friend when he was being teased, the times he had held the door open for teachers, and the times he had made sure no one was left out during games. He hadn't done those things for an award – he had just wanted to treat people right.

Mrs Patel handed him a certificate. "Respect isn't just about using polite words," she said. "It's about how we treat others in our actions. You, Jordan, have set an example for us all."

Jordan grinned. For the first time, he truly understood what respect for others meant.

# What Does It Mean to Respect Others?

Respecting others is about treating people with kindness, fairness and consideration – no matter who they are. It means:

- Listening when others speak and valuing their opinions.
- Being kind, even when we don't agree with someone.
- Standing up for people who are being mistreated.
- Treating teachers, parents and elders with honour.
- Seeing every person as valuable, no matter their background, abilities or beliefs.

Respecting others doesn't mean we have to be best friends with everyone or agree on everything. But it does mean treating people with dignity.

Take a moment to reflect:

Who is someone I respect, and why?

..................................................................
..................................................................
..................................................................

What is one way I can show more respect to my family or friends?

..................................................................
..................................................................
..................................................................

Have I ever felt disrespected? How did it make me feel?

..................................................................
..................................................................
..................................................................

What is something I can do this week to show respect to someone I don't usually talk to?

..................................................................
..................................................................
..................................................................

# A LESSON FROM HISTORY:
## The Story of Rosa Parks

In 1955, a woman named Rosa Parks made a choice that changed history. In Alabama, at the time, there were rules that treated black people unfairly. On a bus ride home, Rosa Parks was asked to give up her seat simply because of the colour of her skin. She refused – because she knew that every person deserves to be treated with respect.

Her act of quiet bravery sparked the Montgomery Bus Boycott, a movement that helped bring change. Rosa Parks didn't shout or fight; she stood firm in her belief that all people deserve dignity.

Her story teaches us that respect isn't just about manners – it's about recognising the worth of every human being. When we respect others, we stand for what is right, just like Rosa Parks did.

# Did You Know?

## MEERKATS AND TEAMWORK

Did you know that meerkats take turns acting as "babysitters" and lookouts to protect their group?

Meerkats live in groups called **mobs** or **clans**, and they survive by working together. While some meerkats go hunting, others **stay behind to care for the young**. They don't just babysit – they also **teach** the younger meerkats how to find food and avoid danger.

Meerkats also **stand on their hind legs and scan the area for predators** like eagles and snakes. If they see a threat, they let out a **special alarm call** so the whole group can hide. Even though the lookout meerkat is in danger by staying exposed, it **respects and protects its family** first.

Just like meerkats, we show respect for others by **helping, teaching and looking out for them**.

CHAPTER THREE

# THE GREATEST ECHO
## Respect for...God

> *The fear of the Lord is the beginning of wisdom."*

Proverbs 9:10, The Bible

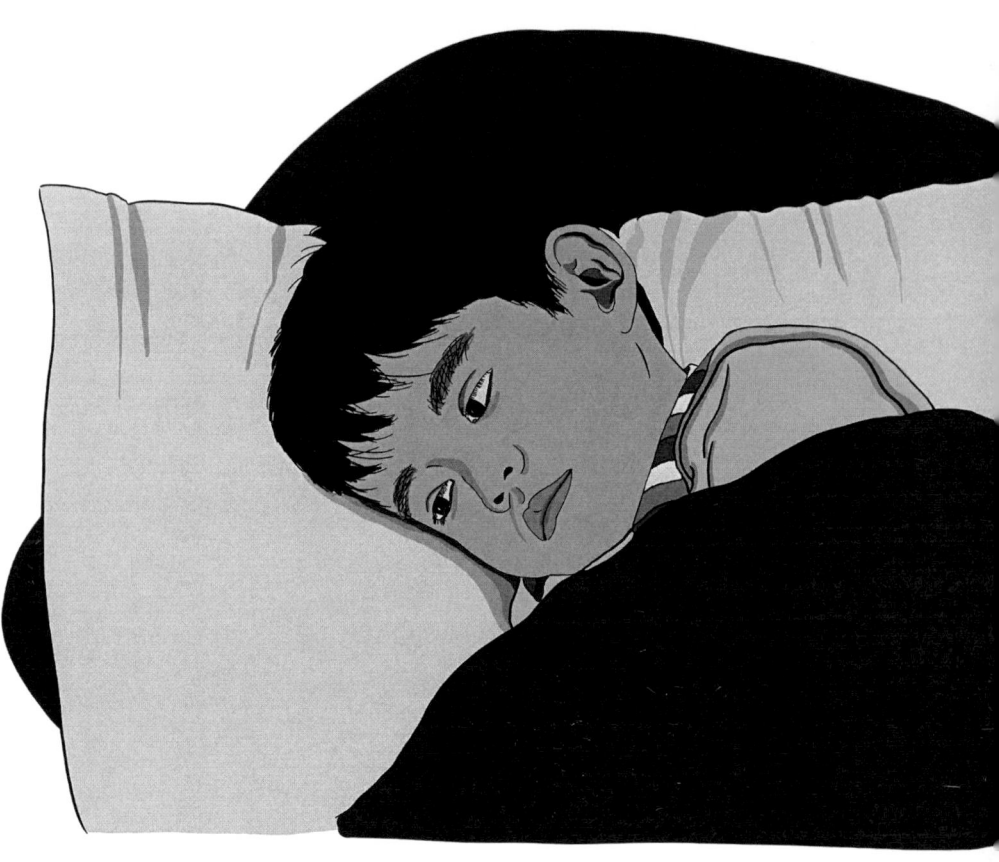

Noah lay in bed, staring at the ceiling. His mum had just kissed him goodnight, but something was still on his mind.

That afternoon, his best friend Jake had told him something surprising.

"I pray every night before bed," Jake had said. "It helps me feel close to God."

## The Greatest Echo

Noah had never really prayed before. He wasn't even sure what to say. But now, lying in the quiet of his room, he felt like maybe he should try.

He sat up, hesitated for a moment, then folded his hands.

"Um . . . hi, God," he whispered. "I don't really know how to do this. But . . . I just wanted to say thank you for today. And, um, please help my family and my friends. And . . . I guess that's it."

Noah paused, then slowly smiled. It felt strange, but also . . . peaceful.

The next morning, he told Jake about it.

"That's great!" Jake said. "Praying is just talking to God. And since He made everything, He's definitely worth talking to!"

Noah thought about that all day. God made everything – the sun, the stars, the ocean . . . and even him. That meant God deserved the most respect of all.

That night, when Noah prayed again, he didn't feel unsure anymore. He knew he was speaking to the One who created it all.

# The Power of Respecting God

Respecting God means recognising who He is – the Creator of the universe and the One who gives us life. When we honour God, we show that we understand His greatness, His power and His love.

Throughout history, those who respected God were blessed, while those who turned away often faced trouble. The Bible gives us many examples of this.

One famous story is about Pharaoh in Egypt. God sent Moses to tell Pharaoh to let the Israelite people go, but Pharaoh refused to respect God's command. Because of this, Egypt suffered through terrible plagues – water turning to blood, swarms of insects, and even darkness covering the land. But when Pharaoh finally listened and obeyed, things changed.

This story reminds us that respecting God isn't just about words – it's about listening to Him and following His ways.

Now, think about your own life:

How can I show respect for God every day?

..................................................
..................................................
..................................................
..................................................

What are some things I can thank God for today?

..................................................
..................................................
..................................................
..................................................

Who do I know that shows great respect for God? What do they do?

..................................................
..................................................
..................................................
..................................................

God is loving and kind, but He is also powerful. He deserves our highest respect, not just in what we say, but in how we live.

---

## The Caterpillar's Choice

A caterpillar, small and bright,
Wandered in the morning light.
It knew one day it had to stay,
Inside a shell, all tucked away.

"But why?" it thought. "Why must I hide,
Within a space so dark inside?
I love the breeze, the sky so blue –
Why trade it for a prisoned view?"

It heard a whisper, soft yet strong,
"You've had your crawling days so long.
Trust the plan, though strange it seems,
For wings are born from silent dreams."

The caterpillar bowed its head,
And though it filled its heart with dread,
It spun its threads and closed its eyes,
Embracing change, though terrified.

Days went by, the world was still,
No more leaves, no more thrills.
But deep within, unseen, unheard,
A miracle began to stir.

And then one day, from its cocoon,
The shell broke wide, and off it flew.
No longer crawling, low and slow,
The caterpillar let go – and rose.

It soared above, no fear inside,
Respecting all God had designed.
For though the path was wrapped in night,
The day had dawned, and wings took flight.

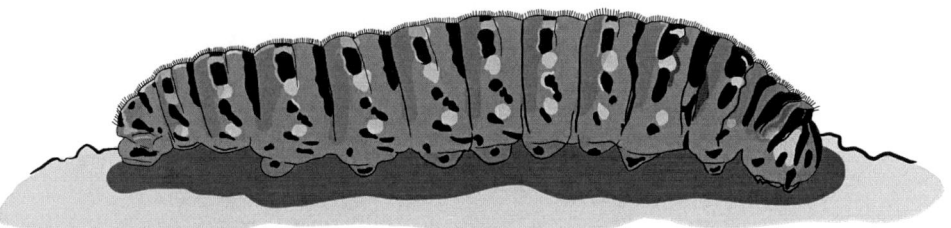

# DEEP DIVE:
## Martin Luther King Jr.

## The Man Who Led with Respect

Martin Luther King Jr. believed that every person deserved to be **treated with respect** – no matter what they looked like or where they came from. But during his lifetime, things weren't fair. In parts of America, black people weren't allowed to use the same buses, schools or restaurants as white people. They weren't treated as equals.

Instead of responding with anger or violence, Martin Luther King Jr. chose a different path. He believed that **real change comes when we treat others with kindness, fairness and respect – even when they don't treat us the same way.**

## Standing Up for Respect

Martin was born in **1929** in the United States. Even as a child, he noticed that black people were treated unfairly. One day, his best friend, who was white, told him they couldn't play together anymore because of the colour of his skin. Martin was heartbroken, but he didn't give up hope that the world could change.

As he grew up, Martin studied hard and became a **pastor**, following in his father's footsteps. He believed that **God created everyone equal** and that the best way to change the world was through **love, respect and peaceful protest.**

He started leading **marches, speeches and protests** – not with fists or anger, but with words and wisdom. He taught people to **fight for justice without fighting each other.**

## The Montgomery Bus Boycott

One of Martin's most famous moments happened in **1955**, when a woman named **Rosa Parks** was arrested for refusing to give up her seat on a bus to a white passenger. At the time, black people were forced to sit at the back of buses and give up their seats if a white person wanted it.

Martin knew this was wrong, so he helped organise the **Montgomery Bus Boycott**. Black people **stopped riding the buses for over a year** to protest unfair rules. Eventually, the law was changed, and buses were no longer allowed to be segregated.

It was proof that standing up for what's right – with **respect, patience and courage** – could lead to real change.

## "I Have a Dream"

One of Martin's most famous moments was his **"I Have a Dream"** speech in 1963. Standing in front of **over 250,000 people** in Washington, D.C., he shared his dream:

*"I have a dream that one day, my four little children will live in a nation where they will not be judged by the colour of their skin, but by the content of their character."*

His words inspired people all over the world to treat each other with kindness and fairness.

## Lessons from Martin Luther King Jr.

Martin Luther King Jr. taught us that **respect can change the world.** Here's what we can learn from his life:

- **Respect others, even when they don't respect you.** He faced anger, threats and even jail – but he never stopped treating others with dignity.

- **Use your words, not your fists.** Martin believed that **peaceful protest** was more powerful than violence.

- **Stand up for what's right.** Even when something feels unfair, we can make a difference **by speaking up with kindness and respect.**

- **Believe in a better world.** Martin's dream of fairness and equality lives on today – and we can all be part of making it come true.

# A Final Thought

Martin Luther King Jr. once said,

*"The time is always right to do what is right."*

Respect isn't just about **what we say – it's about what we do.** Every time we choose to treat others kindly, to stand up for what's right and to believe in fairness, we help make Martin's dream a reality.

How can **you** show respect to others today?

CHAPTER FOUR

# SOUND OF CREATION
## Respect for...my world

> "We do not inherit the
> Earth from our ancestors;
> we borrow it from our children."
>
> Native American Proverb

Oliver pressed his hands against the cool glass of the enormous aquarium, his eyes wide with wonder. Schools of fish shimmered like living rainbows, weaving between towering coral reefs. A sea turtle glided gracefully through the water, its shell a masterpiece of natural design.

"Wow," Oliver whispered. "It's like another world in here."

His class had come to the aquarium on a field trip, and he had never seen anything like this before. The tanks stretched as far as he could see, filled with creatures so colourful and unique that they almost didn't seem real.

"Beautiful, isn't it?" said Mrs Patel, the guide leading the tour.

Oliver nodded. "It's amazing."

Mrs Patel's smile faded slightly as she pointed to a display near the tank. "Do you see that?"

Oliver followed her finger and saw something unexpected – floating pieces of plastic inside a glass case. It looked out of place among all the beautiful sea creatures.

"This is what's happening to our oceans," Mrs Patel explained. "Plastic waste is polluting the water, harming marine life and destroying habitats. That turtle you saw earlier? Many of them mistake plastic for food, and it can make them very sick."

Oliver frowned. "That's awful. I don't want that to happen."

Mrs Patel nodded. "That's why we all have a responsibility to take care of our world. The choices we make – like using less plastic, recycling, and keeping our beaches clean – can help protect these amazing creatures."

Oliver looked back at the sea turtle, watching it swim peacefully. He had always thought of the ocean as something far away, something that didn't really have much to do with him. But now, he realised that everything was connected.

For the first time, he truly understood: respecting the world meant protecting it.

# The Impact of Plastic on Our Oceans

Every year, millions of tons of plastic waste end up in the ocean. It is estimated that:

- **Over 8 million metric tons of plastic** enter the ocean annually.

- **100,000 marine animals** and **1 million seabirds** die each year due to plastic pollution.

- By **2050**, there could be **more plastic than fish** in the ocean if we don't change our habits.

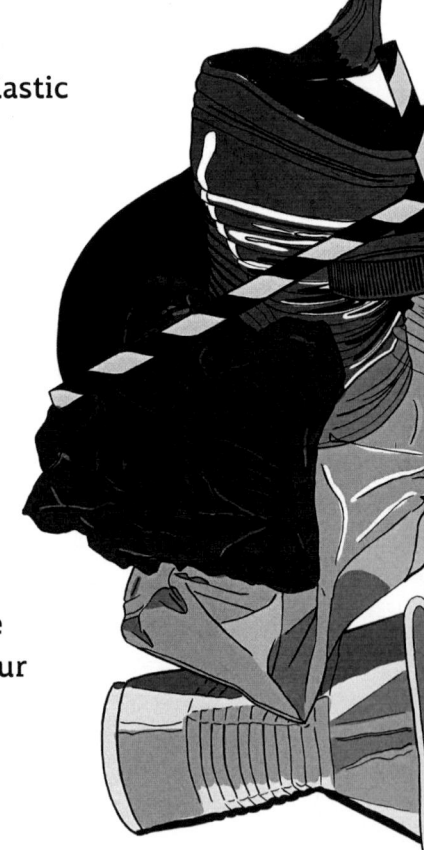

But the good news? We can make a difference!

- How Can I Show Respect for My World?
- **Reduce plastic use.** Say no to plastic straws, bags and bottles when possible.
- **Recycle properly.** Make sure your waste goes into the right bin.
- **Clean up litter.** If you see trash on the ground, pick it up and throw it away.
- **Use reusable items.** Water bottles, shopping bags and containers help reduce waste.
- **Spread awareness.** Encourage friends and family to take care of the environment too!

# Reflect

Think about your own habits and how you can show respect for the world around you.

What is one thing I can do today to help the environment?

How does taking care of nature show respect?

..................................................................
..................................................................
..................................................................
..................................................................

What is one place in nature that I love and want to help protect?

..................................................................
..................................................................
..................................................................
..................................................................

By choosing to respect the world we live in, we are helping to create a cleaner, healthier and more beautiful future – for ourselves and for all the creatures that call this planet home.

# Did You Know?

## THE AMAZON RAINFOREST

Did you know that the Amazon Rainforest produces around 20% of the Earth's oxygen?

This vast rainforest covers **5.5 million square kilometres** (that's about the size of Australia!) and is home to **over 10% of the world's species**. Trees and plants in the Amazon take in **carbon dioxide** and release **oxygen**, helping keep the planet's air clean.

But the Amazon is in danger – **deforestation** means millions of trees are cut down every year. When trees are removed, not only do we lose oxygen production, but carbon dioxide builds up in the atmosphere, making the Earth warmer.

By **recycling, saving paper and protecting forests**, we can show respect for **our planet** – the only home we have!

CHAPTER FIVE

# HANDLE WITH CARE
## Respect for...my belongings

> "Look after the little things and the big things will take care of themselves."
>
> Unknown

Lena groaned as she stared at the mess in her room. Clothes were piled on her chair, books were scattered across the floor, and a plate with crumbs sat on her desk from yesterday's snack.

"Lena," her dad called from the hallway, "it's time to clean your room."

"Do I have to?" Lena sighed. "It's just going to get messy again anyway."

Her dad walked in and surveyed the chaos. "That might be true, but how you take care of what you have now shows how responsible you'll be in the future. Imagine if you had your own house one day – would you want it to look like this?"

Lena shrugged. "I don't know... I guess not."

Her dad smiled. "Let me tell you something important. The way we treat our belongings now shapes our attitude towards bigger things later. If you learn to take care of the little things, you'll be ready for more responsibility when the time comes."

Lena thought about this as she picked up a book and placed it on the shelf. "So, if I take care of my things now, I'll be better at looking after important things in the future?"

"Exactly," her dad nodded. "And besides, respecting your belongings also means respecting yourself. Living in a tidy space helps you think clearly and feel good."

Lena took a deep breath and looked around. Maybe cleaning her room wasn't so bad after all.

# The Power of Respecting Our Belongings

The way we treat our belongings says a lot about our character. If we are careless with what we have, it can lead to wastefulness, frustration and even bad habits. But when we respect our belongings, we show gratitude for what we've been given and develop responsibility for the future.

Think about some of the most successful and trustworthy people in the world. They didn't start with great wealth or huge responsibilities – they proved they could be trusted with little before they were given more.

Jesus told a story that teaches this exact lesson – the Parable of the Talents. In this story, a master gives his three servants different amounts of money to take care of while he is away. Two of the servants respect what they've been given, work hard, and make it grow. But the third servant is careless and does nothing with his share. When the master returns, he rewards the two who used their gifts wisely and takes away the portion of the one who wasted his opportunity.

This teaches us an important truth: if we are faithful with small things, we will be trusted with bigger things.

Take a moment to think about your own belongings.

**What is something I own that I could take better care of?**

..................................................................
..................................................................
..................................................................
..................................................................

**How do I feel when I'm in a tidy, well-organised space?**

..................................................................
..................................................................
..................................................................
..................................................................

**What are some ways I can show respect for my belongings every day?**

..................................................................
..................................................................
..................................................................
..................................................................

When we respect what we have — whether it's our clothes, books, toys or even our home — we show gratitude and responsibility. And as we prove ourselves trustworthy with small things, we open the door for even greater opportunities in the future.

CHAPTER SIX

# ECHO INTO TOMORROW
## Respect for...my future

> *"Do something today that your future self will thank you for."*
>
> Sean Patrick Flanery, actor

# The Echo Effect

Leo loved to stare at the stars.

"One day," he said, lying on the grass with his best friend, Daniel, "I'm going to be an astronaut. Maybe even the first person to play baseball on the moon!"

Daniel chuckled. "That's a pretty big dream."

Leo sat up. "Yeah, but why not? Every big achievement starts as a dream. If I don't respect my future enough to aim high, who will?"

Daniel thought for a moment. "So, what do you do now to make that happen?"

Leo grinned. "Well, I study hard, stay curious, and never stop believing it's possible." He picked up an acorn that had fallen nearby and rolled it in his fingers. "You know, someone once said, 'We ask for oak trees, but God gives us acorns.'"

Daniel raised an eyebrow. "What does that mean?"

"It means the big things we want in life often start small. The question is, will we plant the seed, take care of it and let it grow? If I wait for my dream to happen overnight, I'll be waiting forever. But if I work on it little by little, who knows? Maybe one day, I'll really play baseball on the moon."

# LESSON :
## Respecting Your Dreams

Every great accomplishment in history began as a dream. But dreams need action. Respecting your future means taking care of yourself, making wise choices and believing in your potential.

# The Echo Effect

History is filled with people who dared to dream:

- **Ben and Jerry** wanted to make ice cream that brought people joy – and they did.
- **Mary Anning** discovered dinosaur fossils when people doubted her.
- **Neil Armstrong** looked up at the moon and said, "One day, I'll walk there" – and he did.

But here's the secret: the seeds of your biggest ambitions may already be within your reach. Just like an acorn has the potential to become a mighty oak tree, your dreams – no matter how small they seem today – can grow into something incredible. The question is, will you nurture them?

What are my dreams for the future?
..................................................................
..................................................................
..................................................................

What small steps can I take today to move closer to my goals?
..................................................................
..................................................................
..................................................................

What challenges might I face, and how will I overcome them?
..................................................................
..................................................................
..................................................................

What would I tell a friend who was afraid to chase their dream?
..................................................................
..................................................................
..................................................................

**Remember:** Respect your dreams. Plant the seeds today and, with time and effort, they will grow into something greater than you ever imagined.

"All men dream: but not equally. Those who dream by night in the dusty recesses of their minds wake in the day to find it was vanity, but the dreamers of the day are dangerous men, for they may act their dreams with open eyes, to make it possible."

T.E. Lawrence, *Seven Pillars of Wisdom*

# Did You Know?

## HOW CATERPILLARS BECOME BUTTERFLIES

**Did you know that when a caterpillar becomes a butterfly, it completely changes inside its cocoon?**

Many people think a caterpillar simply **grows wings**, but that's not true! Once inside its **chrysalis**, the caterpillar releases **enzymes** that **break down its entire body** into a liquid-like form. It then **rebuilds itself** into a completely new creature – a butterfly!

This process, called **metamorphosis**, shows us that change isn't instant – it takes time, patience and effort. Respecting our future means making **small choices today** that will **shape who we become tomorrow.**

CHAPTER SEVEN

# BREAKING THE ECHO
## Respect...when I feel disrespected

> "Do not repay anyone evil for evil. Be careful to do what is right in the eyes of everyone."
>
> Romans 12:17, The Bible

# The Echo Effect

Tyler stared at his phone, his stomach twisting into a knot. Someone had left a nasty comment under the video he'd posted the night before. *"You're such a loser. Don't ever sing again."*

His face burned. He wanted to type back something even meaner. That would show them.

At school the next day, he told his friend Josh. "I'm gonna roast this guy. Nobody talks to me like that."

Josh shook his head. "But then you're just giving him what he wants. That's exactly how the echo keeps going — someone disrespects you, you echo it back, and round and round it goes."

Tyler frowned. "So what am I supposed to do, just ignore it?"

"Not ignore," Josh said. "Break the echo. Respond with respect, even when you don't feel like it."

Tyler thought about that. It didn't sound easy. But maybe, just maybe, it would make the echo die out instead of grow louder.

# Breaking the Cycle

We all know what it feels like to be disrespected. Someone rolls their eyes, whispers behind our back, posts a cruel comment online or in a whatsapp group. The temptation is to throw the disrespect straight back — louder, harsher, nastier.

But Jesus taught something completely different. In Luke 6:27–28 He said: *"Love your enemies, do good to those who hate you, bless those who curse you, pray for those who mistreat you."*

That doesn't mean letting people walk all over us. It means choosing not to let their behaviour control ours. Respect is strongest when it's tested.

When we "break the echo," we stop the cycle of insult and revenge. Instead, we send out a different sound — one that builds peace instead of more conflict.

Time to reflect:

**What's one time I felt disrespected recently?**

................................................................
................................................................
................................................................
................................................................

**How did I respond — and how could I break the echo next time?**

................................................................
................................................................
................................................................
................................................................

**Who's one person I can choose to respect, even if they haven't respected me?**

................................................................
................................................................
................................................................
................................................................

## Did You Know?

### THE 90-SECOND RULE

Scientists say that when we feel angry, the physical reaction in our brain and body lasts only about **90 seconds**.

After that, the feelings fade — unless we keep feeding them by replaying the insult in our mind.

That means we actually get to **choose** whether anger controls us or not. Breaking the echo often starts with waiting out those 90 seconds, then deciding to respond with respect instead.

Here are 6 practical ways you can spend your 90 seconds:

1. **Take 10 deep breaths** — in through your nose, out through your mouth. (That's about 90 seconds of calming your body.)

2. **Walk to get a drink of water** — by the time you sip and come back, the first wave of anger has passed.

3. **Listen to your favourite song chorus** — most choruses are around a minute and a half.

4. **Write down what you're feeling** — grab a scrap of paper, jot down the angry words, then crumple it up.

5. **Look out the window and name five things you see** — clouds, trees, birds, cars. It refocuses your mind.

6. **Say a quick prayer** — "God, help me respond with respect." Even a short prayer repeated a few times fills the 90 seconds.

The Echo Effect

# A Lesson from Jackie Robinson
## The Baseball Player Who Broke Barriers

In 1947, Jackie Robinson became the first African-American to play Major League Baseball. But breaking that barrier came at a cost. Crowds shouted insults. Opponents tried to trip him. Some teammates refused to even sit next to him.

Jackie had every reason to throw the disrespect back. But instead, he chose self-control. He let his talent, hard work, and character do the talking. Over time, his example changed the game — and the nation.

Jackie showed the world that breaking the echo of disrespect isn't weakness. It's strength.

## Start a New Sound

Respect isn't just for easy days. It's for hard days, too.

When someone disrespects you, you face a choice: echo it back and make the noise louder, or break the echo and start a new sound.

Like Jackie Robinson - and like Jesus - you can show strength by choosing respect, even when it's the last thing you feel like giving.

CHAPTER EIGHT

# WORDS THAT ECHO
## Respect...in what I say

> "Kind words can be short and easy to speak, but their echoes are truly endless."

Mother Teresa, Catholic missionary

## The Echo Effect

Maya was the class clown. She loved making people laugh, and most of the time her jokes were harmless.

But one day, during lunch, she spotted her friend Liam walking by with a new haircut. Without thinking, she blurted out, "Hey Liam, did a lawnmower attack your head?"

The whole table roared with laughter. Everyone, that is, except Liam. His smile disappeared as he quickly sat down, pulling his hood over his head.

Maya froze. She hadn't meant to be mean — it just slipped out. But words can't be taken back once spoken. That night, Maya lay awake wishing she could rewind time and swallow that joke.

The next morning, she found Liam by the lockers. "Hey," she said quietly, "about what I said yesterday... I'm really sorry. It was supposed to be a joke, but it wasn't funny. I hurt you."

Liam hesitated, then gave a small smile. "Yeah, it stung. But thanks for saying sorry. I forgive you."

Maya learned that words have echoes we can't always control — but respect gives us the chance to start a new echo, one filled with healing and hope.

# Words That Stick

Our words are powerful. They can build someone up with encouragement, or they can tear someone down with criticism.

That's why Proverbs 18:21 says, *"The tongue has the power of life and death."*

Think about it:

- A single kind word can give someone courage to keep going.
- A single cruel word can echo in someone's heart for years.
- A sincere apology can soften the sharpest echo and begin to heal what was broken.

Respect isn't just about what we do — it's about what we *say*. Every word we speak leaves an echo. The question is: what kind of echo do you want to leave behind?

---

# 16,000 Words A Day

On average, each of us speaks about **16,000 words every single day**. That's like filling up a whole book... every 24 hours!

By the end of a week, you've "written" the same number of words as the entire first *Harry Potter* book. By the end of a year, you've spoken more than **60 novels' worth of words!**

And that's just spoken words. Add in texts, social media posts, and voice notes, and the number is even higher. We're constantly creating a trail of echoes with what we say and write.

Scientists say our brains are wired to remember **negative words more strongly than positive ones** — meaning a harsh comment can sting longer than a kind one. That's why encouragement is so powerful: it balances out the weight of negativity and helps people flourish.

The words themselves might disappear from the air in seconds, but their **echo in someone's heart and mind can last for years.**

That's why every word is a choice. Will my daily "book" be full of words that encourage, or words that hurt?

Time to reflect:

What kind words have been spoken to me recently?

........................................................................
........................................................................
........................................................................
........................................................................

What's a word I wish I could take back — and how might I make it right?

........................................................................
........................................................................
........................................................................
........................................................................

If my words are going to echo today, what do I want them to sound like?

........................................................................
........................................................................
........................................................................
........................................................................

# The Power of Peaceful Words

Desmond Tutu was a South African bishop and human rights leader who became a global voice for justice. He grew up during a time when laws of apartheid treated people of different races unfairly — separating schools, neighbourhoods, and even park benches. It was a world full of angry echoes — insults, lies, and rules that divided people.

But instead of adding more anger, Tutu chose a different sound. He used words of peace, justice, and respect. His speeches and sermons gave people hope when life felt hopeless. He reminded his country — and the world — that forgiveness is stronger than revenge.

Tutu didn't just fight against what was wrong; he painted a vision of what could be right: a "rainbow nation" where people of every background could live together in dignity. For this, he was awarded the Nobel Peace Prize in 1984.

His words didn't just echo in South Africa — they reached across the globe. Desmond Tutu gave the world an example of how respectful words can carry the power of life, hope, and healing.

# Echo Check

Maya learned that even a quick joke can wound someone's heart.

We all get to choose our words. Will they echo with kindness, courage, and life? Or will they echo with hurt, anger, and shame?

Respect means paying attention to what comes out of our mouths. Because once words are spoken, the echo is out there — and it can travel further than we ever imagine.

CHAPTER NINE

# HONOUR UP
## Respect...for those who lead and care for us

> "Respect is earned, honesty is appreciated, trust is gained, and loyalty is returned."

Unknown proverb

# The Echo Effect

Ellie had been in Mrs Patel's class for almost a whole year. Every day, Mrs Patel patiently explained maths problems, organised group projects, and even stayed behind after school to help students who were struggling.

But Ellie never really thought much about it. Teachers were just ... teachers. It was their job, right?

One afternoon, Ellie stayed late to grab her bag and noticed Mrs Patel still tidying the classroom. For the first time, she saw the tired look on her teacher's face.

"Mrs Patel?" Ellie asked. "Why do you always stay so late?"

Mrs Patel smiled. "Because you're all worth it."

Ellie went home thinking about those words. The next day she wrote a simple note: *"Thank you for caring about us."* When she slipped it onto Mrs Patel's desk, her teacher's eyes filled with tears.

Ellie realised something powerful: showing honour doesn't take much, but it means the world to those who give so much.

## Honouring Doesn't Mean Blind Obedience

Respecting leaders, parents, or teachers doesn't mean agreeing with everything they say or do. It doesn't mean ignoring mistakes or pretending they're perfect.

Honour is about recognising the weight of responsibility they carry, and choosing to treat them with dignity and respect.

The Bible says in Romans 13:7, *"Give to everyone what you owe them... if respect, then respect; if honour, then honour."*

When we honour those who lead and care for us, we help create a culture of encouragement — one where leaders, carers, and teachers don't burn out, but keep going because they know they're valued.

Time to reflect:

**Who's one person I often take for granted?**

..................................................................
..................................................................
..................................................................

**What's one way I could show honour to them this week?**

..................................................................
..................................................................
..................................................................

**How would my school, home, or community change if everyone chose to show honour?**

..................................................................
..................................................................
..................................................................

## Did You Know?

### RESPECT FOR THE AGED DAY

In Japan, there's a national holiday called Respect for the Aged Day.

Every September, people celebrate older generations with parades, ceremonies, and special meals. Children visit their grandparents, communities give gifts, and TV programmes honour the oldest citizens.

It's a reminder that honouring those who came before us is not old-fashioned — it's a sign of strength and gratitude.

# Practical Ways to Show Honour

- Write a thank-you note to a teacher, carer, or coach.
- Offer to help at home without being asked.
- Speak politely, even when you don't feel like it.
- Stand up when an elder walks into the room.
- Pray for leaders in your school, church, and community.

Honour doesn't have to be complicated — just consistent.

# A Lesson from Bear Grylls
## Adventurer, Explorer, and Man of Faith

Bear Grylls is known for climbing mountains, crossing deserts, and surviving in the wild. But in interviews, he often says that respect and honour are just as important as courage.

He talks openly about honouring his family, his faith in God, and the leaders who have guided him. He even served in the British Special Forces, where honour and respect were the foundation of teamwork.

Bear's adventures prove that strength isn't only about survival skills. It's also about valuing the people who lead, care, and support us.

## Honour That Echoes

Ellie learned that a simple note of thanks could mean more than she ever imagined.

Honour may feel small, but its echo is huge. It encourages leaders, strengthens families, and inspires communities.

And the best part? Anyone can do it — starting today.

# A Final Word on Respect

Respect is more than just good manners or polite words — it's a way of living that shapes how we see ourselves, how we treat others, and how we interact with the world around us.

Throughout this book, we've explored different ways to show respect:

- **Respect for myself** — Because how we see and treat ourselves sets the foundation for everything else in life.

- **Respect for others** — Because kindness, empathy, and fairness make our relationships stronger.

- **Respect for God** — Because He created us, and honouring Him leads us toward wisdom and purpose.

- **Respect for my world** — Because we only have one planet, and it's up to us to take care of it.

- **Respect for my belongings** — Because appreciating what we have teaches us responsibility and gratitude.

- **Respect for my future** — Because every dream starts small, and what we invest in today shapes our tomorrow.

- **Respect when I feel disrespected** — Because breaking the echo of anger or insult takes courage and creates peace.

- **Respect in what I say** — Because words carry weight, and their echoes can build up or tear down.

- **Respect for those who lead and care for us** — Because honour encourages, strengthens, and reminds others that their work matters.

Respect isn't always easy. It takes patience, effort, and sometimes even a change of perspective. But when we live with respect, we not only improve our own lives — we make the world a better place for everyone.

So the question is . . . **what kind of echo will you choose to leave today?**

# TO PARENTS AND TEACHERS:
## Helping Young People Level Up

Dear Parents and Teachers,

Thank you for choosing the *Level Up* series to invest in the next generation. These books were written with a clear goal: to help young people discover and develop core values that will shape their lives from the inside out.

Each chapter is built around real-life stories, fun metaphors, faith-based inspiration and practical examples that children can relate to. To get the most out of these books, here are a few simple ways you can bring the content to life:

## For Parents:

- **Bedtime conversations** – Read a chapter together and use it as a springboard for open, meaningful discussion.

- **Car chats** – Use chapter titles or questions as prompts during drives or while waiting in queues.

- **Celebrate growth** – When your child shows curiosity, confidence, respect or potential in action, call it out and cheer them on!

## For Teachers:

- **Small group discussions** – Use chapters to spark class conversations, circle time or Personal/Social/Health sessions.

- **Curriculum connections** – Many chapters link naturally with Religious Education, citizenship or literacy themes.

- **Creative response activities** – Invite students to write, draw or present their own take on a chapter's theme.

Whether you're reading with one child or a whole class, our hope is that these books will inspire a journey of growth – and give you the joy of walking that journey together.

Let's raise a generation ready to level up!

# soul ⊛ children

# SOUL CHILDREN UK:
## Sing. Grow. Belong.

Do your children love to sing? Are you looking for a way to help them grow in confidence, creativity and community?

**Soul Children UK** is part of an international network of youth gospel choirs that gives children aged 9–16 a place to belong and a voice to be heard. Through high-energy rehearsals, powerful songs and inspiring performances, Soul Children helps young people discover who they are – and who they're becoming.

## A message for teachers:

Thinking about starting a choir in your school or community? Soul Children UK provides everything you need:

- Songs kids love to sing
- Simple resources and support
- Training and encouragement for leaders
- A network of choirs across the UK – and beyond!

Whether you're a seasoned music teacher or just passionate about helping young people grow, you don't have to do it alone.

**Visit soulchildrenuk.com** to learn more, hear the music and join the movement.

# worshiphouse KiDS

## Ready to
# SING, DANCE, AND DIVE
### Deeper into Chip's Level Up Series?

**Meet AAA** – Access All Areas – the creative geniuses behind the songs, games, and all-out fun inspired by the values in Chip's book!

🎵 Jam out to kid-approved songs that bring the Bible to life

💃 Dance your heart out with easy-to-follow videos

🎲 Play Bible Story Bingo & flex those Scripture smarts

📱 Scan that lil' QR code to explore the full collection on WorshipHouse Kids.

Let's keep **learning, laughing, and lifting** up His name—together (with some serious style, of course).

# WANT CHIP TO VISIT YOUR SCHOOL OR CHURCH?

Hi, I'm Chip — author of the Level Up series. I love visiting schools and churches to talk about the values behind these books—things like confidence, potential, respect, and curiosity.

My sessions are packed with stories, games, real-life examples, and practical ways to live out what we learn. Sometimes I even bring my sound system and sing a song or two!

Whether it's for an assembly, classroom session, youth group, or Sunday service, I'd love to be part of what you're doing to inspire the next generation.

Want to find out more?

Email: bookings@chipkendall.com

Let's start the conversation!

# READY FOR MORE?

You've reached the end of the book...

...but this is just the beginning of your Level Up journey!

Head over to levelupbooks.com to explore:

**More Titles** – Explore the rest of the Level Up series and find your next favourite book

**Bonus Material** – Activities, videos, downloads, and more to help you level up in real life

**Bulk Purchase Offers** – Perfect for schools, churches, and youth groups

**Contact & Booking Info** – Want Chip to visit your school or church? You'll find everything you need

**Join the Mailing List** – Be the first to hear about new releases, sneak peeks, and exclusive extras!

Let's keep growing, learning, and becoming the people we were made to be.

One choice at a time.
One level at a time.

Let's Level Up!

# CHECK OUT THE FULL LEVEL UP SERIES

**The Courage Code** – Level Up Your Confidence
ISBN 978-1-917455-30-5

**The Silent Spark** – Level Up Your Potential
ISBN 978-1-917455-27-5

**The Echo Effect** – Level Up Your Respect
ISBN 978-1-917455-28-2

**The Wonder Switch** – Level Up Your Curiosity
ISBN 978-1-917455-29-9